YOUR KNOWLEDGE HAS VALUE

Bibliographic information published by the German National Library:

The German National Library lists this publication in the National Bibliography; detailed bibliographic data are available on the Internet at http://dnb.dnb.de .

Imprint:

Copyright © 2017 GRIN Verlag
Print and binding: Books on Demand GmbH, Norderstedt Germany
ISBN: 9783668621985

This book at GRIN:

https://www.grin.com/document/387298

Simon Kaguru

Design and Implementation of a web-based University Voting Sytem

GRIN Verlag

GRIN - Your knowledge has value

Since its foundation in 1998, GRIN has specialized in publishing academic texts by students, college teachers and other academics as e-book and printed book. The website www.grin.com is an ideal platform for presenting term papers, final papers, scientific essays, dissertations and specialist books.

Visit us on the internet:

http://www.grin.com/

http://www.facebook.com/grincom

http://www.twitter.com/grin_com

UNIVERSITY VOTING SYSTEM

(UVS)

SIMON KIIRU KAGURU

A RESEARCH PROJECT SUBMITTED IN PARTIAL FULFILLMENT OF THE REQUIREMENTS FOR THE AWARD OF BACHELOR OF SCIENCE IN INFORMATION SCIENCES TO MOI UNIVERSITY

2017

ACKNOWLEDGEMENTS

I am greatly indebted to a number of people without whose assistance and input this project could not be a success.

First of all, I acknowledge the power of Almighty God, who has always been present to give me the strength and inspiration to keep on working and complete this study.

To my parents and siblings, thank you for your continuous support, unconditional love and encouragement.

To my supervisor, Mr. Evans Munge for the dedication and professional guidance offered to me during the research process. Great thanks to all the lecturers and other staff members who have assisted me during the course of my studies and also throughout the project implementation period.

DEDICATION

This research project report is dedicated to my Dad and Mom whose support has enabled me to complete it. To my sisters Rachel, Lucy and Mary and my brothers, Joram and Daniel, thank you for your continued support.

TABLE OF CONTENTS

Table of Contents

LIST OF FIGURES

LIST OF TABLES

ACRONYMS

UVS	University Voting System
GUI	Graphical User Interface
ICT	Information Communication Technology
CUE	Commission for University Education
IASAS	International Association of Student Affairs and Services

ABSTRACT

An Online Voting System is a web based system that facilitates the running of elections online. Most higher learning institutions in Kenya conduct elections regularly in order to elect a student leadership to elect them. The elections conducted are mainly manual hence they are marred with irregularities which usually affect negatively the results of the election. In this era of advanced technology where online systems boosts work speed, reduces mistakes and promote the generation of accurate results, having a manual system like the paper-based version becomes a misfortune. An online system, which involves procedures like registration of voters, vote casting, vote counting, and declaring results etc. would constitute a good solution to replace current system that is in the universities in Kenya. Online systems have the advantage of providing convenience to the voter and reduce the time wasted in the queuing process at election centers and also promote security in the voting process. This paper hence describes the UVS which is a web-based online voting system that helps facilitate voting on the internet by providing a platform students are provided with an online registration form which requires them to register as voters, and then the details filled on the form are submitted in the database which then approves the user who can then login into the UVS and cast their vote. The UVS was developed using the waterfall model due to the adaptive nature of web based applications and the system proved that a computerized solution is possible with elimination of human related faults that are a commonplace in employment of human clerks to manage the election process. This paper has proposed the basic structure of the system and its functionality which can be employed to replace the current electoral system used in Universities.

CHAPTER ONE

INTRODUCTION

1.1 Background of the study

Kenya has a large number of universities and other institutions of higher learning. There are 22 public universities, 14 chartered private universities and 13 universities with Letter of Interim Authority (LIA) (CUE, 2014). These universities are established through institutional Acts of Parliament under the Universities Act (2012) which provides for the development of university education, the establishment, accreditation and governance of universities.

For any democracy to prevail in any form of leadership public opinion is the most important determinant to establish leadership and voting is the process through which people display their opinion and help to setup a democratically elected leadership. Most Universities student bodies in developed countries including Ivy League universities have implemented online voting systems that ensure free, fair, transparency and credibility in elections. In Kenyan Universities however, the process of voting has always been the paper-based voting which has always been marred with irregularities resulting in abrupt riots by students. Throughout history, election fraud has occurred in many electoral processes from which experience shows that the manual voting process is a major source of such vices and violence in many democratic countries as well as in Universities.

The International Association of Student Affairs and Services (IASAS) is currently an informal confederation of higher education student affairs/services professionals from around the world. A number of its members have been actively engaged for some time in

1

defining the need for, and organization of, an international community of student affairs and services professionals.

Student's bodies play a vital role in the operations of any successful learning institution. It is an organization being politically uninvolved, legally required to serve the entire student community at a given higher education institution (Amirianzadeh, Jaafari, Ghourchian & Jowkar, 2011). These organs appoint their representatives to work in collective bodies of the given higher education institutions. In Kenya, students unions involve themselves not only in university politics, but also in national politics. Most of the student organizations in Kenyan Universities are guided by the national values of governance, principles of leadership and integrity as spelt out in Article 10 of the Constitution of Kenya (2010). This ensures that they have a share of governing the operations of the learning institution in order to ensure that they secure themselves and our posterity academic freedom, excellence, liberty and our welfare.

The authority and responsibilities of various leaders in the student organizations vary according to their various institutions. For example, the president who is always the leader of the student organization in a particular university serves as spokesperson of the entire student body. The president may oversee his or her association's efforts on student activity events and planning, school policy support from students, budget allocation, fiscal planning, and recognition of developing issues pertaining to students, and communication between faculty/staff and the student body.

In this regard, the existence of a University Voting System (UVS) that ensures integrity of votes casted is a requirement that should be implemented by the Universities in Kenya. Online Voting or E-voting will ensure that elections are held free and fair and that results are transmitted to voters in a secure way better than the paper-based system of voting. Online voting is a term encompassing several different types of voting embracing both electronic means of counting votes. Online voting, by contrast, is predicated on privacy, anonymity, and freedom from outside influence or coercion—but also on the absolute audit ability that is necessary to guarantee the principle of "one person, one vote" and to verify that each voter's intent is reflected in the election's outcome (Kohno, Stubblefield, Ribin & Wallach, 2004).

The UVS is geared towards increased the voting percentage in most of the Kenyan university and to reduce occurrences of irregularities such as voter bribery, ballot-stuffing, manipulation of votes and rigging and also replace the old paper-based voting method which is far from perfect.

The advantage of online voting over the common "queue method" is that the voters have the choice of voting at their own free time and there is reduced congestion. It also minimizes on errors of vote counting. It also ensures that paper ballots cannot be lost, stolen, or destroyed, and voters cannot be coerced on site. The individual votes are submitted in a database which can be queried to find out who of the candidates for a given post has the highest number of votes (Shamos, 2004).

The UVS requires that students should first register as voters before been authorized to vote. The registration should be done prior to the voting date to enable data update in the database. For an individual to be able to participate as a voter, they should be currently enrolled in a program in the institution that has implemented the online voting system. When registering as a voter, an individual should fill out details including the admission number whereby the online voting system will liaise with the database storing the registration details of students in the particular learning institution. This should be able to keep off individuals who are not students in the University that is carrying out the voting process.

1.2 Problem Statement

The voting/polling process by voters in Kenyan Universities is very cumbersome. Some of the voting processes, mainly in public universities are influenced by external forces such as ethnic division as is the occurrence in the national general elections in Kenya. This leads to malpractices in the election process that usually results in chaos and violence in some of the public universities. This has resulted in the enactment of bills in the Kenyan National Assembly that seeks to regulate the voting process in Kenyan learning institutions. The paper-based system of voting has resulted in elections that are marred with violence which evidently reflect the process of voting not only in universities, but also nationally.

The UVS should be able to bridge this gap and bring credibility in the process of voting in Kenyan Universities. Cases of voter bribery, ballot staffing, manipulation of votes and rigging can be avoided by implementing the online voting system. Such cases can be solved by insisting on voters to exercise that task online using the online voting system.

1.3 Aim of the Project

This project report is aimed at illustrating, elaborating and discussing how the UVS has been developed and to also explain how the system can be utilized in Kenyan Universities and Colleges.

1.4 Objectives of the project

The main objectives of this report documentation are the following:

- Reviewing the existing/current voting processes and systems or approach in Universities

- To elaborate and discuss in detail the functions of the different technologies used in the development of the system

- To provide a detailed overview of the user interface of the web application as seen by the end user through illustrations.

- To illustrate the system design that has been used in the development of the system

- To investigate user requirements for a web based voting portal

- To provide a ground for further research into this field and enrich the academia.

1.5 Objectives of the system

- Coming up with an automated voting system for Kenyan Universities

- Implementing a an automated/online voting system

- Providing students with a reliable voting system that can be easily accessed through the internet.

- Ensure security in the registration of voters and the anonymity of voters.

- Validating the system to ensure that only eligible voters are allowed to vote.

- To provide a system that automatically tallies cast votes for individual candidates

- To provide a system that archives summarized reports and statistics with regard to the conduct of an election process

1.6 Significance of the Project

The importance of the UVS is to ensure provision of improved voting services to the voters through fast, timely and convenient voting. The UVS should also be able to reduce the costs incurred by the paper-based voting system and also the workload that accompanies the hiring of clerks in the voting process. The UVS should be able to manage the elections effectively and ensure that security standards are functioning in an effective manner in order to deliver a credible election. The UVS is also important because it will increase the number of voters participating in the election as individuals will find it easier and more convenient to vote as the system will not restrict voters to cast their vote in different locations.

1.7 Project Justification

The UVS is a system developed with current technologies and a robust database system. The UVS shall be able to ensure credibility in the voting process in Kenyan Universities unlike the paper-based voting system which is always marred with multiple irregularities. The UVS shall reduce the time spend making long queues at the polling stations during voting. Cases of vote miscounts or spoilt votes shall also be solved since at the backend of this system resides a well developed database system using MySQL that can provide the correct data once it's correctly queried.

1.8 Scope of Study

The scope is focused on studying the existing system that solves the same porblem as the USV does. The study will produce less effort and less labor intensive, as the primary cost and focus primary on creating, managing, and running a secure web voting portal.

1.9 Limitation of Study

Time factor was the greatest barrier to the successful completion of this exercise since it had to be done within the semester. I also had financial constraints since all the activities involved were self-sponsored.

CHAPTER TWO

LITERATURE REVIEW

2.1 Introduction

The advancement in technology in recent years, where online systems boosts work speed, reduces mistakes and promote the generation of accurate results, having a manual voting system becomes a misfortune (Aziz, 2011). With the onset of technology and computers, computerized processes have been invented world over to improve efficiency and credibility of voting processes. Two distinct approaches in computerized voting processes are electronic voting and online voting. While online voting aims to provide a web based interface via which voters can cast their votes and get results of the election process, electronic voting has to do with the registration process being carried out electronically e.g. use of biometrics and coded voter cards that that can be scanned by an electronic device to authenticate the voter. Thus, an electronic voting system may end up having human clerks tallying the votes upon termination of the election process (Emaase, 2011).

Online voting and electronic have become the technologies that most democracies and also universities in the 21st century are using. Voting on the internet has its own disadvantages based on the areas of secrecy and protection against coercion and/or vote selling. In Kenyan universities, only a few of them have tried to implement voting via the internet but they have not been successful on designing a standalone voting system customized for the particular university. According to the Elections journal of British Columbia District, Canada, online voting refers to a voting method that transmits voted ballots via the public Internet through a web browser or client application accessed through an internet-connected personal computer, smart phone or tablet.

In an article titled "Why America Can't vote online" it states that Canada and Estonia are among the pioneers of online voting, with the town of Markham, in Ontario, having offered online ballots in local elections since 2003 (Anand & Pallavi, 2012).

David Chaum (2004) advocates for a process, whereby voters could get receipts for their votes. This receipt would allow them to verify whether their votes were included in the final tally or not, and to prove that they voted without revealing any information about how they voted. The inclusion of this improves credibility in the election process and anonymity of voters. He suggests that e-voting is technologically viable with application of cryptography and security reinforcement algorithms.

Matt Schultz and Tom Miller (2012) protested that database matching in online voting processes had loopholes as illegal voters managed to get registered. This is a challenge that comes when a system provides online registration and should be well addressed to ensure such incidences never occur. The duo proposes a personal identity number to uniquely identify each voter and facilitate cross checking. Their insight was therefore of great aide in the design considerations of the UVS. Dr. Michael Shamos (1993) presents Six Commandments summary of requirements for a voting which though similar to others' requirements, he maintains himself as less afraid of the catastrophic failures and sweeping fraud made possible by imperfections in electronic voting machines. Shamos is also much less impressed with paper ballots. He places a great deal of faith in decentralization to make fraud difficult to commit and easy to detect. Online voting should be a solution to curb the challenge of cheating in elections and provide a baseline for online voting system as that such a system should provide a high level of security and establish five core requirements of an electronic voting system to address issues of privacy, authentication, anonymous, uniqueness and coercion (Kalaichelvi & Chandrasekaran, 2012). University of

9

Texas [A&M University] online voting system shows that web technologies can be harnessed to facilitate voting processes and one no longer needs to be physically at the Campus setting to exercise their democratic right as a student. The system exposes a web interface via which students log in and cast their votes during the electioneering period (Nzoka & Ananda, 2015). In Kenya, universities and colleges have to rely on the human clerk electoral processes. Online voting replaces some of the traditional methods of voting that are still being used in modern day by some countries and colleges across the world

The methods can be divided into five;

1. **Paper-based voting:** The voter gets a blank ballot and use a pen or a marker to indicate he want to vote for which candidate. Hand-counted ballots is a time and labor consuming process, but it is easy to manufacture paper ballots and the ballots can be retained for verifying, this type is still the most common way to vote.

2. **Lever voting machine**: Lever machine is peculiar equipment, and each lever is assigned for a corresponding candidate. The voter pulls the lever to poll for his favorite candidate. This kind of voting machine can count up the ballots automatically. Because its interface is not user-friendly enough, giving some training to voters is necessary.

3. **Direct recording electronic voting machine**: This type, which is abbreviated to DRE, integrates with keyboard; touch screen, or buttons for the voter press to poll. Some of them lay in voting records and counting the votes is very quickly. But the other DRE without keep voting records are doubted about its accuracy.

4. **Punch card**: The voter uses metallic hole-punch to punch a hole on the blank ballot. It can count votes automatically, but if the voter's perforation is incomplete, the result is probably determined wrongfully.

5. **Optical voting machine**: After each voter fills a circle correspond to their favorite candidate on the blank ballot, this machine selects the darkest mark on each ballot for the vote then computes the total result. This kind of machine counts up ballots rapidly. However, if the voter fills over the circle, it will lead to the error result of optical-scan.

2.2 Case Study: Easwari Engineering College Voting System

An online voting system is a web-based that facilitates the running of elections and surveys online. Users are individuals who interact with the system. All user interaction is performed remotely through the user's web browser. Users are provided with an online registration form before voting user should fill online form and submit details these details are compared with details in the schools database and if they match then user is provided with username and password using this information user can login and vote. If conditions are not correct entry will be canceled. It contains two level of user's administrator level and voter level where each level has different functionality.

2.2.1 System Background

The system is developed to provide users with a simple and self explanatory Graphic User Interface (GUI). Users are supposed to register and login in the system then pick their favorable candidates to register his vote.

11

Online voting system is a voting system by which any Voter can use his/her voting rights from anywhere in country. Online voting system contains:

a) Voter's information in database.
b) Voter's Names with ID and password.
c) Voter's vote in a database.
d) Calculation of total number of votes.

Various operational works proposed in the system are: Recording information of the Voter in database. Checking of information filled by voter. Discard the false information. Each information is sent to administrator.

2.2.2 System Workaround

Remote users are eligible to access and exercise voting in the Easwari College Voting System. Results can be viewed by the administrator without counting the votes cast. All the counting is computerized.

2.2.3 Product Functions

The product has a server back-end which takes care of authenticating the users and maintaining necessary data structures.

2.2.4 Overview of Data Requirements

The internal memory requirement will be constant or linearly dependent on the number of users depending on the provision of changing the vote at a later time. The external data about the candidates

2.2.5 Constraints

Login and password is used for identification of Voter.

2.2.6 Features on the System

Online voting is software system through which a voter can give votes through registering themselves on the voting website. all the information in sites which has been entered are stored in database for each page in the website have its own database table. It deals with design, build and test the online voting system that facilitates user

2.2.6.1 Home

It is the welcome page of the website, having all the feature options of the website.

Figure 1 Homepage

2.2.6.2 Registration

This is the register page, where the voter, candidate and can register themselves. They all have to enter basic information best of their known .All the information registered in the website are saved in the respective database not require geographical proximity of the voters. For example, soldiers abroad can participate in elections by voting online.

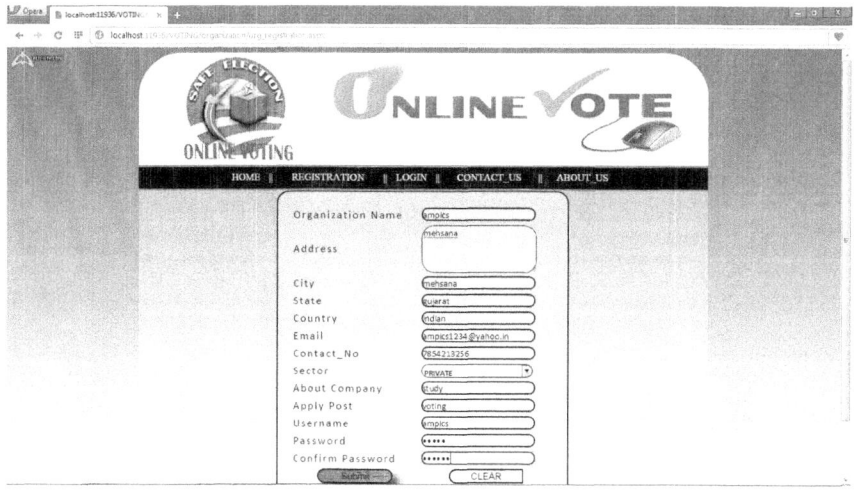

Figure 2. Voter Registration Page

2.2.6.3 Login

User Login: After registering into the website, this information is saved to the database and sent

to the election commission. The user can Login to the website with his unique USERNAME and

PASSWORD generated through registration. There is a option for FORGOT PASSWORD, in

case user forget his password then he/she can go with option of forgot password.

Candidate Login: After registration candidate can see his/her profile and can edit his/her

profile. The candidate has facilitated with all the latest news update regarding election.

Figure 3. Login Page

CHAPTER THREE

RESEARCH METHODOLOGY

3.1 Introduction

In this chapter, the libraries, algorithms and the data structures used are presented. It includes specific methods which were used in order to achieve the objectives of the system, particular requirements for implementation of the system and a brief explanation of why such methods were used for implementing the system. It also shows how the system was implemented and also explains how the program works.

3.2 System Overview

UVS is an online web system to be used for voting by universities in Kenya. It can be able to register, tally and count individual votes casted by students in a particular university. The system's main function is to conduct an election of student leaders using the internet to allow students to vote. The UVS can be able to run on any computer or mobile device which is connected to the internet. The system will liaise with the university's student registration details in order to ensure that only bonafide students are eligible to vote in the polls. The system should also be integrated with the schools website to allow ease of access by students. The UVS will only function when there are open elections.

A student who would like to vote will be directed to the system through the universities website. Here, he/she will be asked to register and then login to the system. If the details used for registration are correct, the system will load to the homepage. The student should be brought to the homepage when logged in. The student can view other pages which are the current polls and the profile management page.

If a student wishes to vote, he/she should click the current polls page which lists the available positions which are available for voters to vote. The student should choose the position, then the person he/she is voting for in that particular post. Once the vote confirmed, the vote will be transmitted over the internet to a central server. The administrator is the only one who is allowed to view how the voters have cast their votes without displaying their names in order to ensure anonymity. The votes for the candidates will be tabulated and the vote information will be printed out.

3.3 System Analysis

This section will offer a description of the existing system, derive its limitations and also provide an in depth description on the proposed UVS system. It will also lay out the targeted objectives of the proposed system. The section will also look at the differences between the existing system and the proposed system and also describe its feasibility study.

3.3.1 Existing System

The existing system is paper-based voting which is highly manual. In most of the Kenyan Universities, voters usually use their school identity cards for the verification of the voters. Usually, there is no any form of registration of voters prior to the election date. An election date is usually set by the student organizations officials with support from the universitys administration. Verification is done manually by clerks who usually ask voters for their school identification cards. After verification by the clerk, the voter goes ahead to pick the ballot paper which contains the name of the canditate and sometimes, his/her photo. The voter then drops the ballot paper inside the ballot boxes.

18

Tallying of the votes is also done manually by counting the votes that were cast one by one. The returning officer announces the results by announcing to the students who has ganered more votes than the other in the various posts. The votes are usually recorded in paper format for reference purposes.

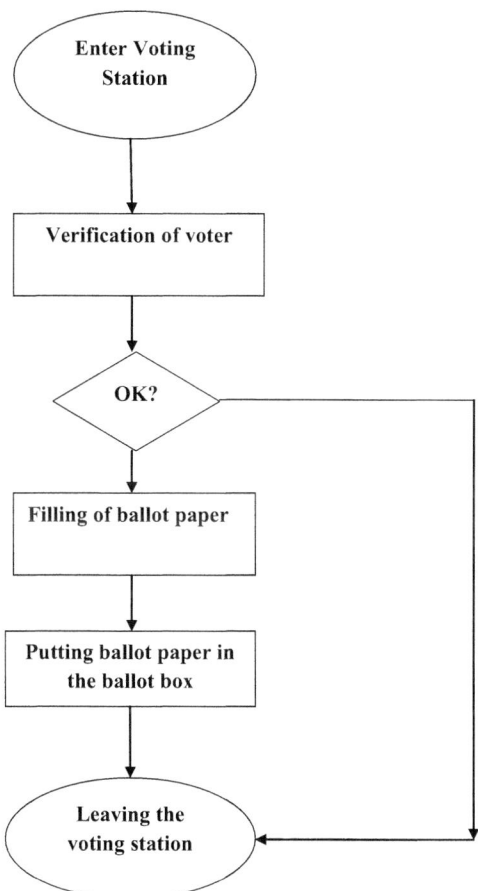

Figure 4. Existing system voting process

3.3.2 Limitations of the Existing System

The problems of the existing manual system of voting include among others the following:

1. Expensive and Time consuming: The process of printing ballot papers and also filling the details of various candidates names takes too much time and is expensive to conduct.

2. Too much paper work: The process involves too much paper work and paper storage which is difficult as papers become bulky with the population size.

3. Errors during data entry: Errors are part of all human beings; it is very unlikely for humans to be 100 percent efficient in data entry.

4. Loss of ballot papers: Some times, ballot papers get lost in the process of preparing them hence sometimes some students do not vote due to the shortage of ballot papers.

5. Manual systems are very subject to voter error and that could potentially lead to fraud acts by various candidates.

6. Short time provided to view the voter register: This is a very big problem since not all people have free time during the given short period of time to check and update the voter register.

7. Above all, a number of voters end up being locked out from voting.

Hence there is great desire to reduce official procedure in the current voter registration process if the general electoral process is to improve.

3.3.3 Proposed System

In the proposed voting system, everything from registration of voters, verification of voters, casting of the votes and tallying is done online. The system will be a web based information system that enables individuals to cast their vote only once. All the information filled in when registering as a voter is stored in a database.

The main objective of the UVS is to ensure that all the limitations that exists in the manual voting system are dealt with accordingly. The UVS will ensure that ID verification is carried out as it will liaise with the university registration database to ensure that students with a valid ID cards are the only ones who are eligible to participate in the elections.

3.3.3.1Objectives of the Proposed System
Objectives of the system

- Coming up with an automated voting system for Kenyan Universities
- Implementing a an automated/online voting system
- Providing students with a reliable voting system that can be easily accessed through the internet.
- Ensure security in the registration of voters and the anonymity of voters.
- Validating the system to ensure that only eligible voters are allowed to vote.
- To provide a system that automatically tallies cast votes for individual candidates
- To provide a system that archives summarized reports and statistics with regard to the conduct of an election process

3.4 System Requirements
Several tools were used in the development of the UVS to ensure that voting is conducted through the internet. The web-based UVS was developed as an online information system to offer users convenient access to the voter register.

3.4.1 Technologies
Various types of software were used in order to implement the UVS.

3.4.1.1 XAMPP

XAMPP is a free open source cross-platform web server package developed by Apache Friends. XAMPP stands for Cross Platform (X) Apache (A), MariaDB (M), PHP (P) and Perl (P). It is a simple, lightweight Apache distribution that makes it extremely easy for developers to create a local web server for testing and deployment purposes. Everything needed to set up a web server – server application (Apache), database (MariaDB), and scripting language (PHP) – is included in an extractable file. XAMPP is also cross-platform, which means it works equally well on Linux, Mac and Windows. Since most actual web server deployments use the same components as XAMPP, it makes transitioning from a local test server to a live server extremely easy as well. The UVS was developed and tested locally on a windows computer.

- **Apache**

Apache Web Server is a very stable and robust web server for the Linux, Unix, Windows and other related operating systems that existed today. Apache is a process-based structure, the process consumes more system costs than the thread does, so it is not suitable for multi-processor environment, therefore, when an Apache Web site needs to expand, usually to increase or expand a server cluster rather than increase processors.

Apache Architecture

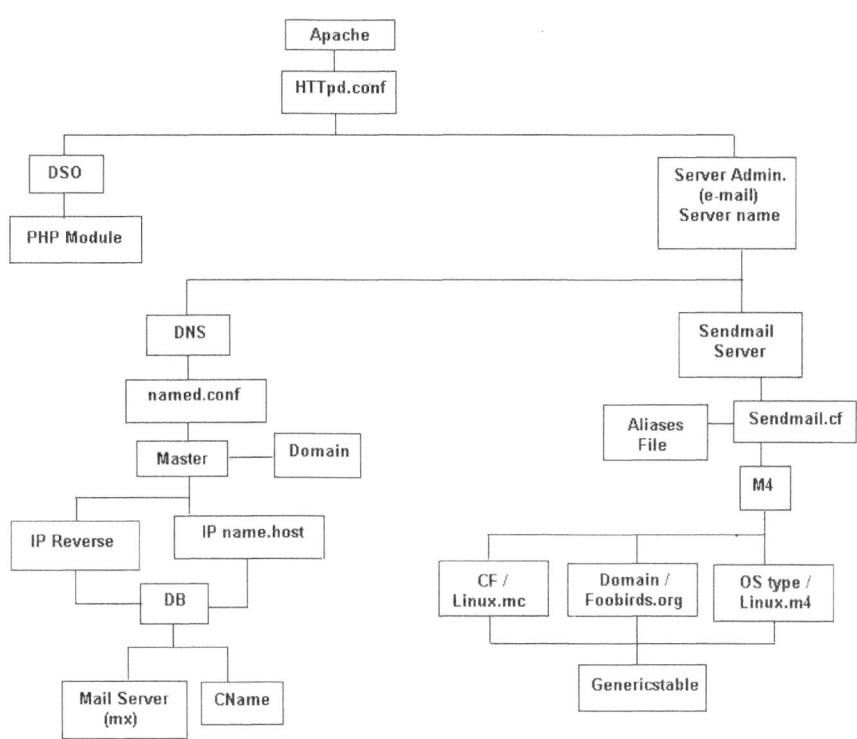

Figure 5. Apache Achitecture SOURCE: Zhang, 2010

- **MySQL DBMS**

MySQL is a popular relational database management system. It can provide high performance and stability. It is used by websites developers to build different types web applications, it provides API for many languages such as: C, C++, Java and PHP etc. The top layer of MySQL architecture is not unique for MySQL, all network-based C/S for web applications should include the connection handling, authentication, security management. The middle layer is the core of MySQL, including query parsing, analysis, optimization, and caching. It also provides functions across storage engines, including stored procedures, triggers and views and so on. The bottom layer is a storage engine, which is responsible for access to data. Web server through the storage engine API can interact with a variety of storage engines.

- **PHP**

PHP: Hypertext Preprocessor is a webpage programming language that was designed to produce dynamic web pages. For this purpose, PHP code is embedded into the html source file with PHP tags and interpreted by a web server. PHP's special syntax mixes C, Java, Perl syntax. It can be faster than the CGI or Perl when implements dynamic webpages.

The following is PHP architecture. The top layer is web serve which will process PHP code, middle layer is PHP core which provides most important PHP api, such as connection to database, under it is zend api and extensions, the bottom layer is zend engine which used as php compiler and executor.

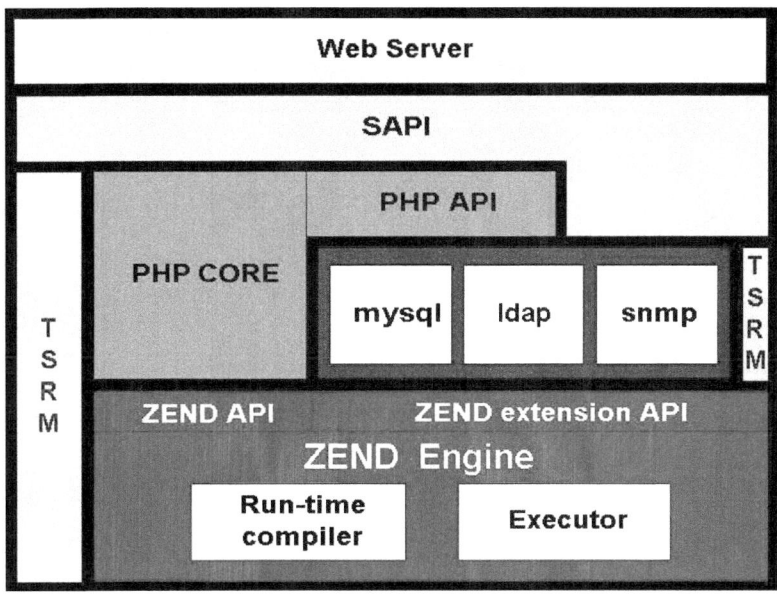

Figure 6. PHP Architecture SOURCE: Zhang, 2010

- **Perl**

Perl is a programming language developed by Larry Wall, especially designed for text

processing. It stands for Practical Extraction and Report Language. It runs on a variety of

platforms, such as Windows, Mac OS, and the various versions of UNIX. Perl is a general-

purpose programming language originally developed for text manipulation and now used for a

wide range of tasks including system administration, web development, network programming,

GUI development, and more.

3.5 Hardware and Software Requirements

The minimum configuration required to run this project are:

Table 1. Hardware Requirements

Hard Disk	40 GB Free Disk Space
RAM	2 GB
Processor	2.0 GHz

Table 2. Software Requirements

Operating System	Windows 7 or other Compatible OS
Front end	HTML, CSS, JavaScript, PHP
Backend	My SQL,
Web- Browsers	Internet Explorer, Mozilla Firefox, Google Chrome, Opera, Safari etc.
Other tools	Notepad ++, Codelobster, Adobe Dreamweaver

3.6 Software Model

A process model for software engineering is choosen based on the nature of the project and application, the methods and tools to be used, and the controls and deliverables that are required. The model is used to build the UVS software is "The Prototyping Model". The prototyping paradigm is: - "Water fall model"

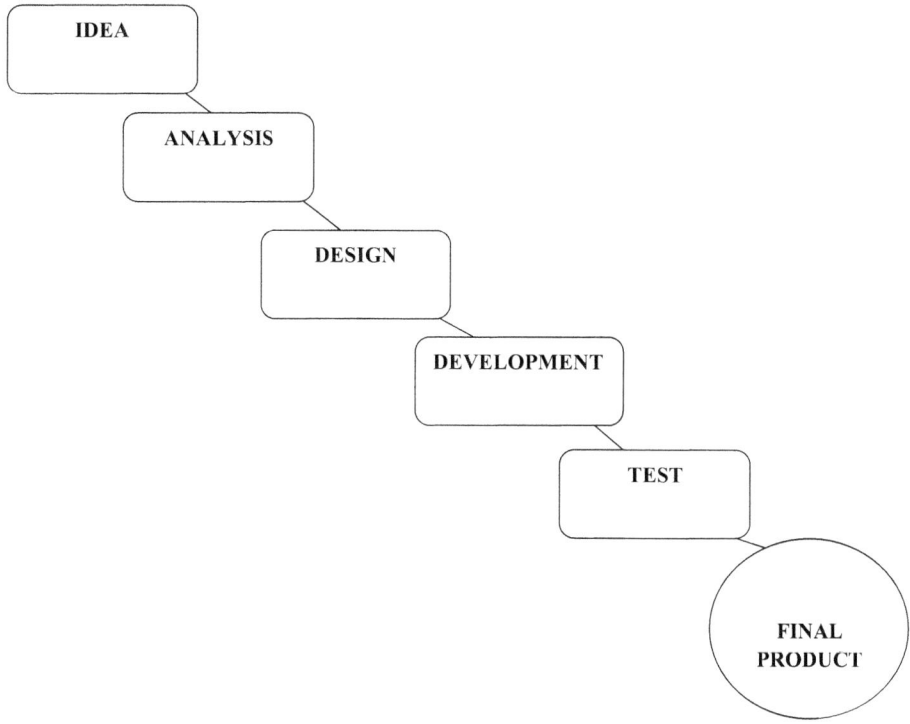

Figure 7. Water fall Model

The water fall model is a software development model in which a systems development is viewed as flowing downwards through the phases of the system development process. The waterfall methodology is powerful, précised, and thorough. It has a number of phases that have to be implemented in a sequential manner.

The phases which come under the waterfall model are as follows:-

1. Requirement Analysis

2. Design

3. Implementation

4. Testing

5. Maintenance

Advantages:

1. Good for large projects

2. Waterfall suits a principled approach to design

3. Waterfall divides the project into manageable areas

4. Waterfall separates the logical and physical

3.7 System Design

The aim of this section is to describe the architecture, modules, interfaces, and data of the UVS to satisfy the laid out requirements. It will outline how the database was designed, the procedures followed and the design constraints that were met during the process of designing the UVS system. It will also be able to define the major software components and their relationships. The UVS is designed to offer its services to two different individuals, the administrator and the users (students).

3.8 Timeline Chart

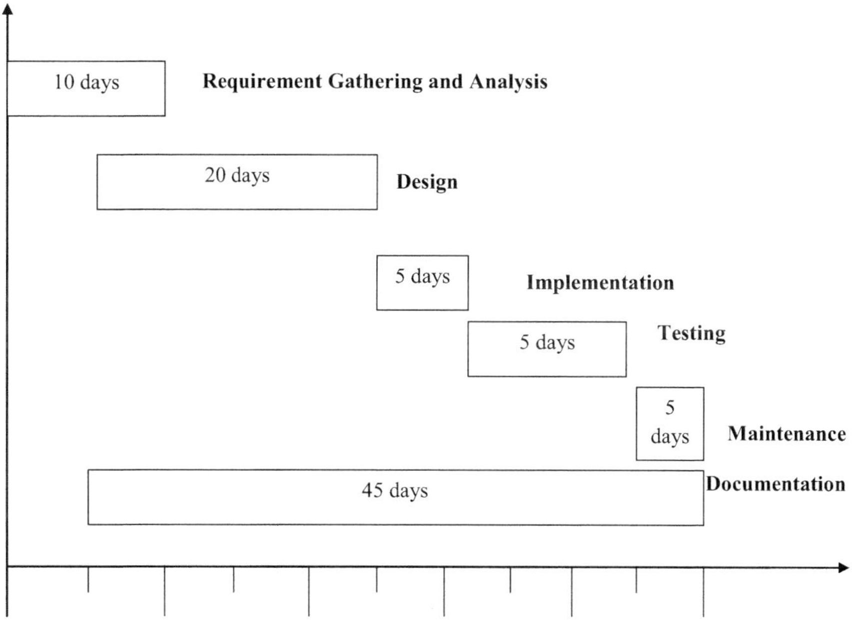

Figure 8. Timeline Chart

3.8 Database Design

Database is very important in an information management system, designing a good database

architecture will directly affect the efficiency of the application system. Reasonable database

structure can improve the efficiency of data storing, to ensure the data integrity and consistence.

The UVS database contains four tables, namely: Administrators, Candidates, Members and

Positions.

3.8.1 Administrators

This table holds the records consisting of the names of the system administrators, their email and

their passwords. An administrator can be able to add more administrators in the administrator

panel.

Table 3. Admin Table

Field name	Data type	Description
Admin ID	Int(5)	Identifies the admin(Primary Key)
First Name	Varchar(45)	Login id for Admin
Last Name	Varchar(45)	Login id for Admin
Email	Varchar(45)	Login id for Admin
Password	Varchar(45)	Password for Login

3.8.2 Candidates

This table holds the records of the candidates ID, candidates name, candidates' position and the number of votes of each candidate. The database is queried to find out how many voters' casts their votes for a given contestant

Table 4. Candidates table

Field name	Data type	Description
Candidates ID	Int(5)	Identifies the candidate(Primary Key)
Candidates name	Varchar(45)	Name of the candidate
Candidates Position	Varchar(45)	The position of the candidate
Candidates votes	Varchar(11)	Number of votes

3.8.3 Members

This table holds the records of the users or voters that are registered into the UVS. The table records the members ID, the first and last name of the voter, the email and the password.

Table 5. Members

Field name	Data type		Description
Members ID	Int(5)	NOT NULL	Identifies the voter (Primary Key)
First name	Varchar(45)	NOT NULL	First name of the voter
Last name	Varchar(45)	NOT NULL	Last name of the vote
Email	Varchar(45)	NOT NULL	Email of the voter
Password	Varchar(45)	NOT NULL	Password of the voter

3.8.4 Positions

This table holds records containing the names of the different positions that candidates are

contesting for.

Table 6. Position table

Field name	Data type		Description
Position ID	Int(5)	NOT NULL	Identifies the position (Primary Key)
Position name	Varchar(45)	NOT NULL	The name of the positon

3.9 Database Entity-Relation (ER) Diagram

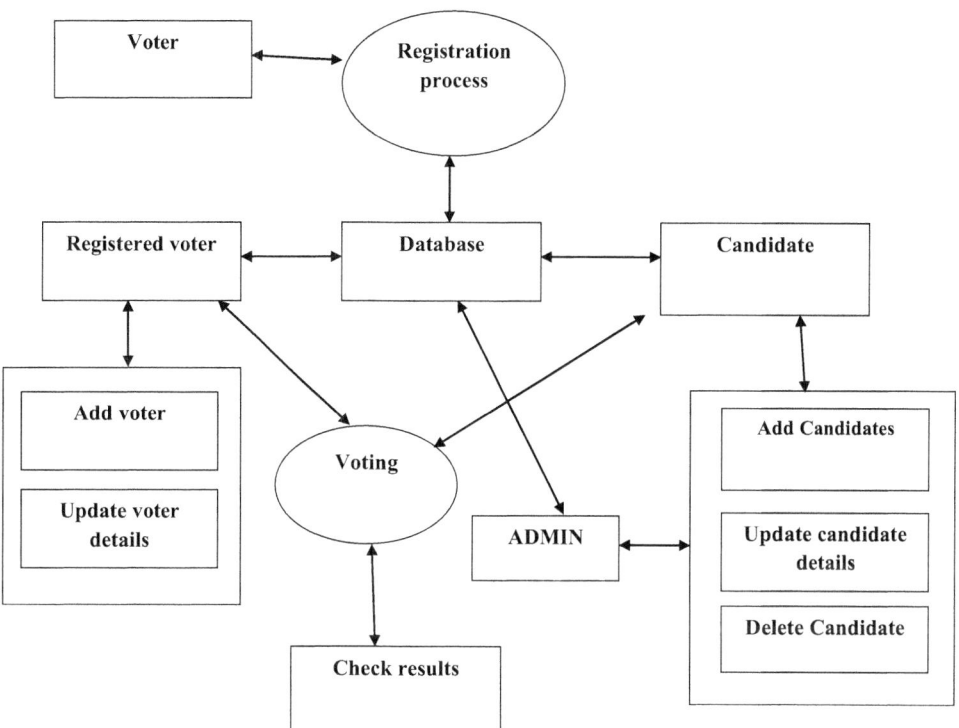

Figure 9. Database Entity-Relation (ER) Diagram

35

3.10 Data Flow Diagram

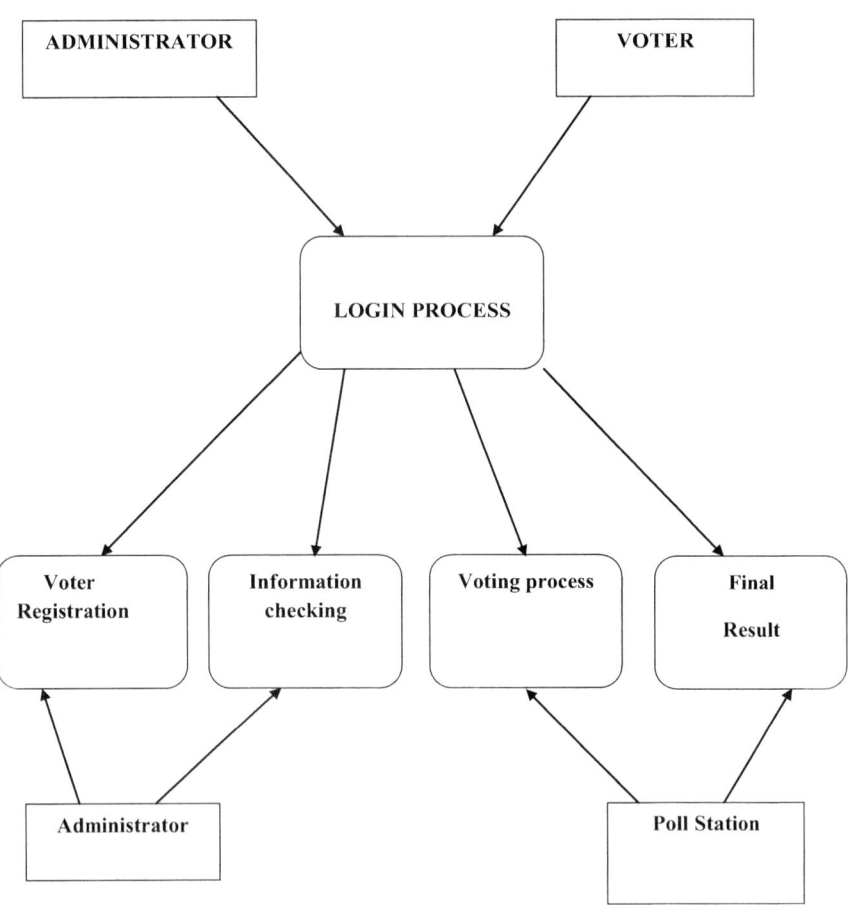

Figure 10. Data Flow Diagram

3.11 Use Case Diagram

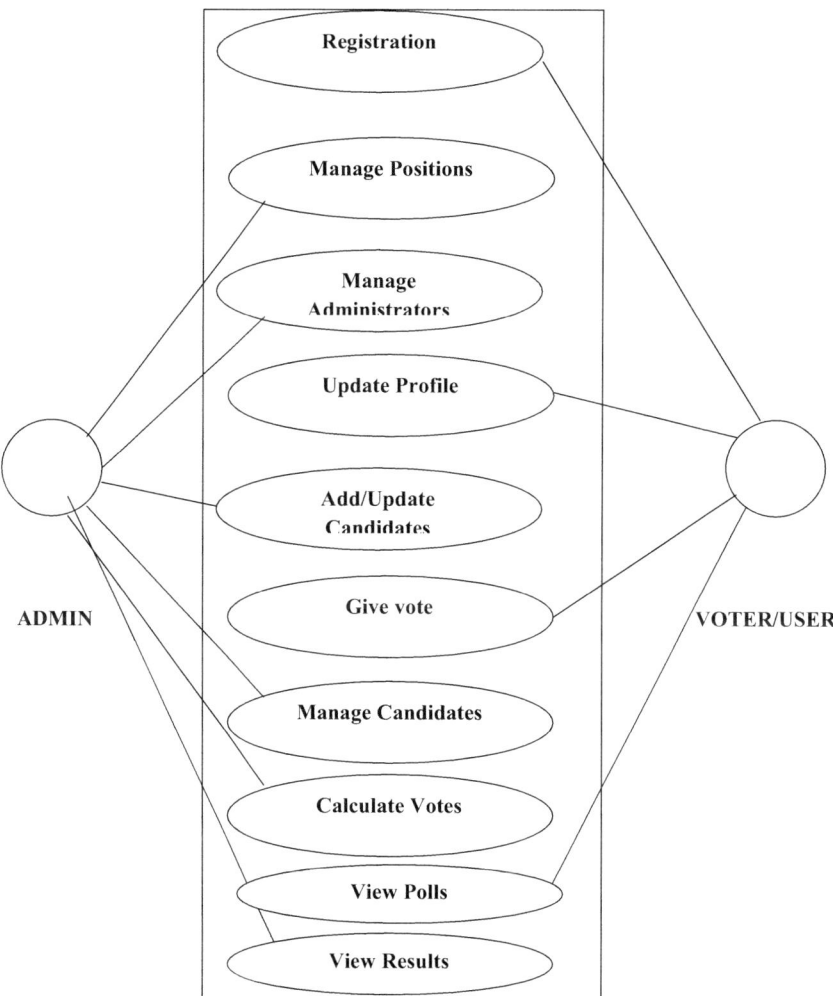

Figure 11. Use Case Diagram

3.12 Activity Diagrams

- **Admin Activity**

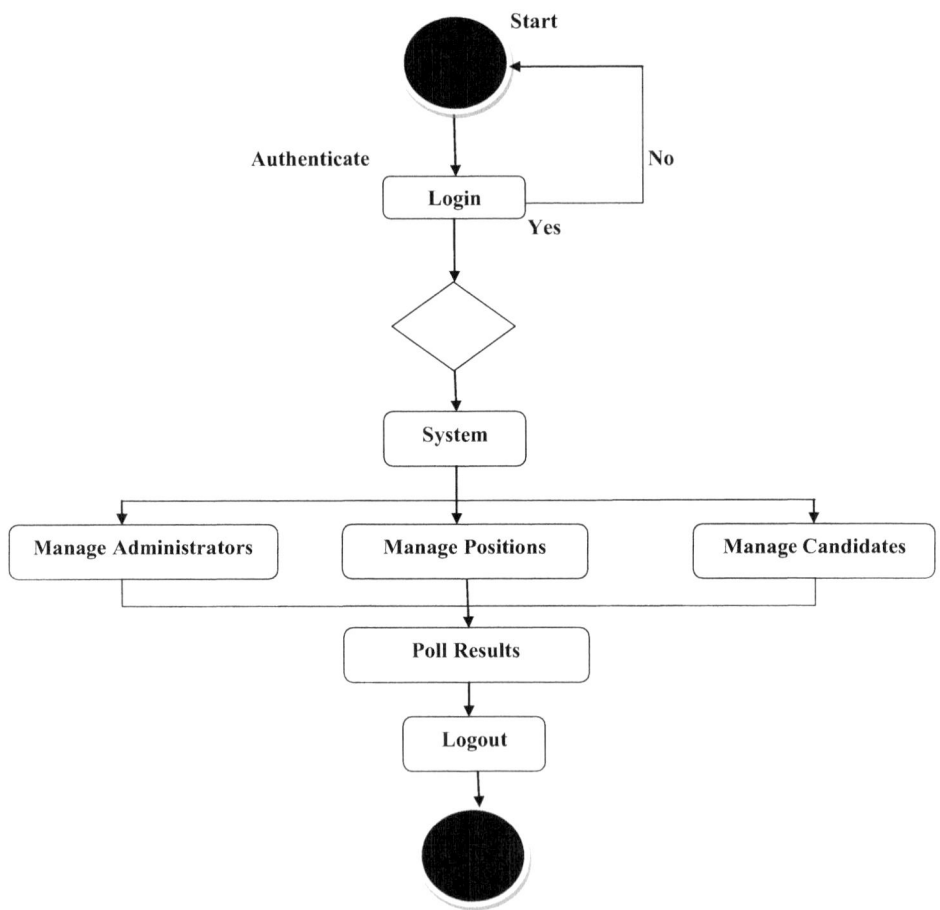

Figure 12. Activity Diagrams: Admin Activity

- **Voter Activity**

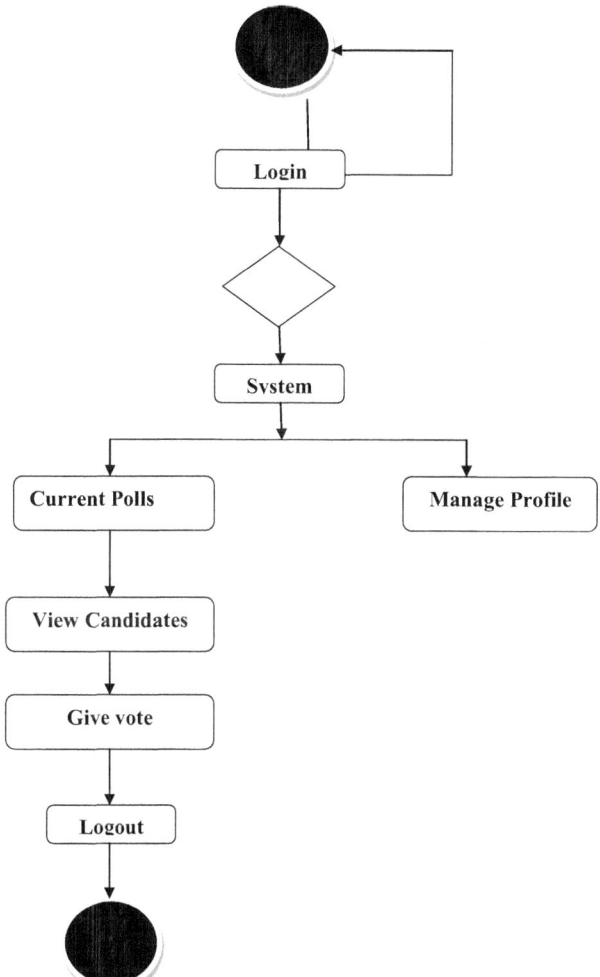

Figure 13. Activity Diagrams: Voter Activity

3.13 System Flow Chart
Admin

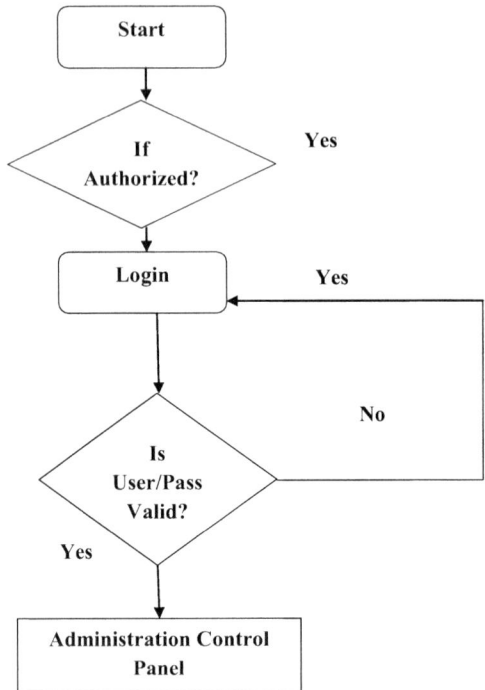

Figure 14. System Flow Chart: Admin

Voter

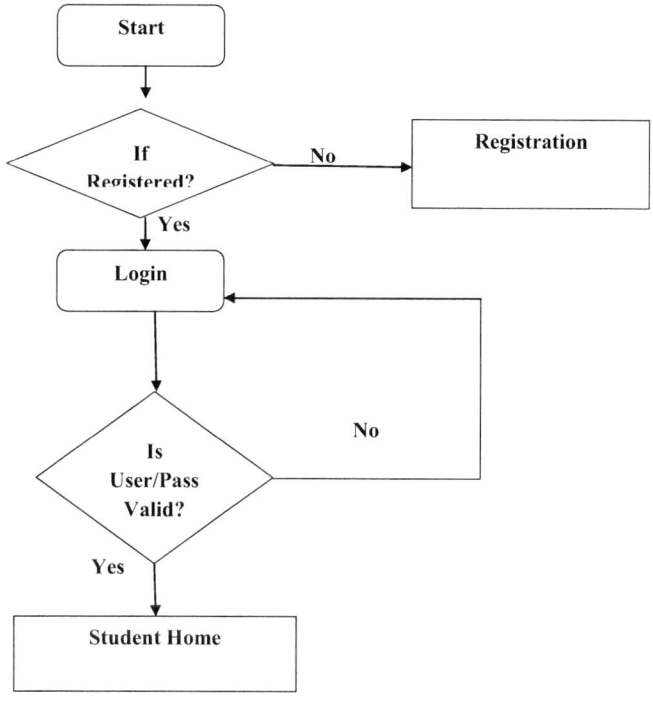

Figure 15. System Flow Chart: Voter

CHAPTER FOUR

TESTING AND RESULTS

4.1 Introduction

Software testing provides manual or automated means used to run or test a system or a process aimed at testing whether it satisfies the specified requirements or expected results. To provide high quality, software system should place emphasis on reliability and integrity. Testing is the process of running a system with the intention of finding errors. Testing enhances the integrity of a system by detecting deviations in design and errors in the system. Testing aims at detecting error-prone areas. This helps in the prevention of errors in a system. Testing also adds value to the product by conforming to the user requirements.

The main purpose of testing is to detect errors and error-prone areas in a system. Testing must be thorough and well-planned. A partially tested system is as bad as an untested system. And the price of an untested and under-tested system is high.

4.2 Form input and Reports Design

The UVS is a system developed to offer an interactive mechanism between the user at the interface and the database using the web-browser. This tool enables a user through a web browser to interact with the MYSQL database to enter, edit, view and retrieve such data as per the privileges granted. These forms were also kept as short and simple as possible for easy public awareness on the use of the tool, some of the forms and report interfaces created include the following:

4.2.1 User/Voter Registration Form

This form can be accessed by students only who have a valid student admissions number. The system administrator can also be able to access the form.

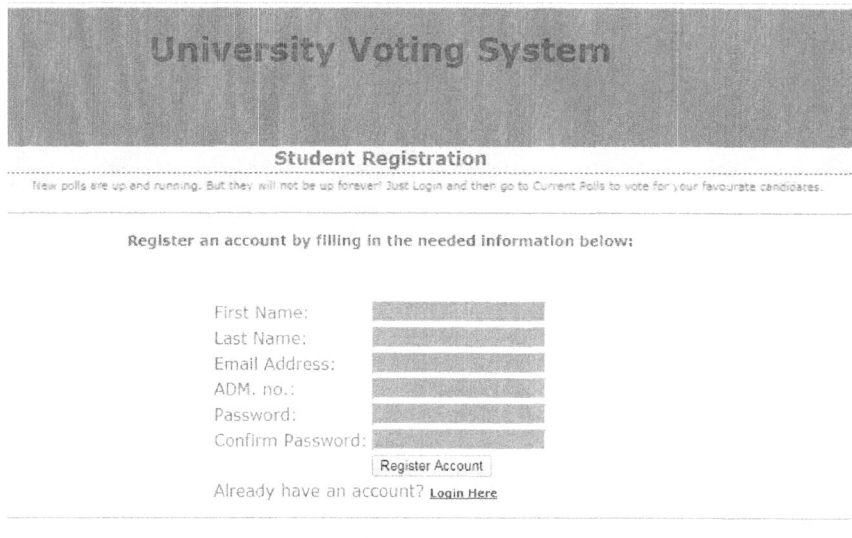

Figure 16. User/Voter Registration Form

4.2.2 User Login Form

This is where a new user/voter starts; the individual is required to provide a username and password which he/she filled in when registering as a voter. When this is provided the system validates the user if the entered information tallies with what is in the database. He/she is then logged in otherwise the voter/user isn't logged in.

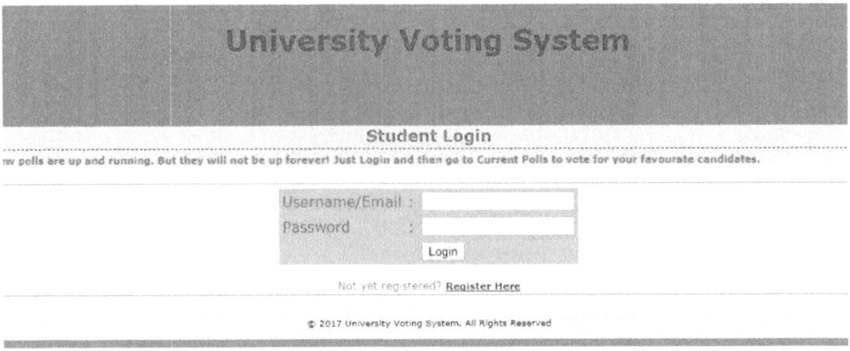

Figure 17. User Login Form

4.3 Testing

The UVS was tested on the Google Chrome web browser by the developer. The developer ensured all the system requirements were available and then the testing commenced. The system was hosted locally in the computer on the Xampp web server.

The key capabilities of the system were put into testing. In this case they included;

- The ability to login into the system as the admin or the user.

- The ability to register as a user.

- The ability to view the current polls and vote as a user.

- The ability to manage the profile as the user.

- The ability to manage administrators as the admin.

- The ability to add and remove positions as the admin.

- The ability to add or remove candidates as the admin.

- The ability to view the poll results as the admin.

All the above functions were put to testing by the developer.

4.3.1 User logged in page

This is the first page that the user/students encounter once he/she is logged into the UVS. It is also the homepage of the user panel.

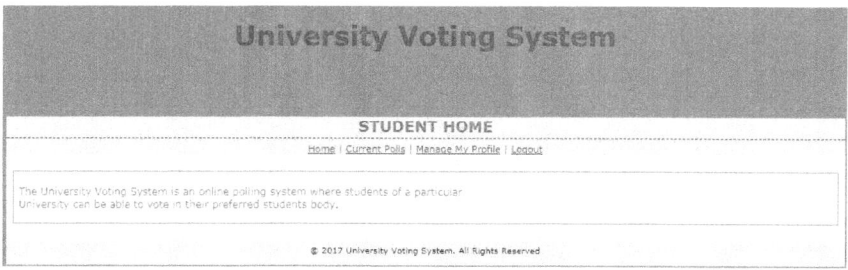

Figure 18. User logged in page

4.3.2 Current Polls Page

This page provides the user with the capability of viewing what polls are available and also acts as the voting page where students can click on a position on the drop down menu and view the candidates, then choose the candidate they would like to vote for.

Figure 19. Current Polls Page

4.3.3 User Profile Management Page

A user of the UVS can be able to manage their profile in this page. It offers functions such as

updating the email address and also changing the password.

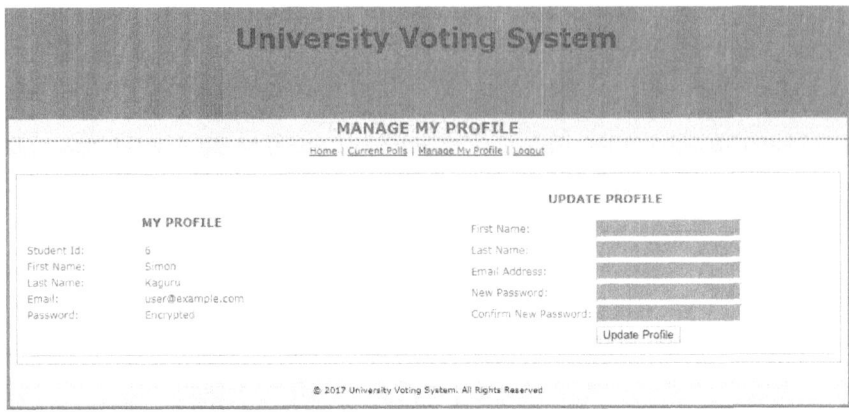

Figure 20. User Profile Management Page

4.3.4 Admin Logged in page

This is the first page that the admin encounters once they login into the UVS.

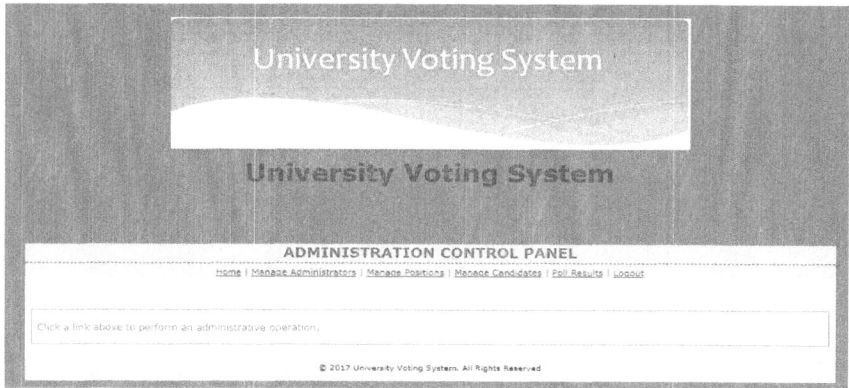

Figure 21. Admin Logged in page

4.3.5 Manage Positions Page

This page ensures that the admin is able to add or remove positions that are to be contested in the election.

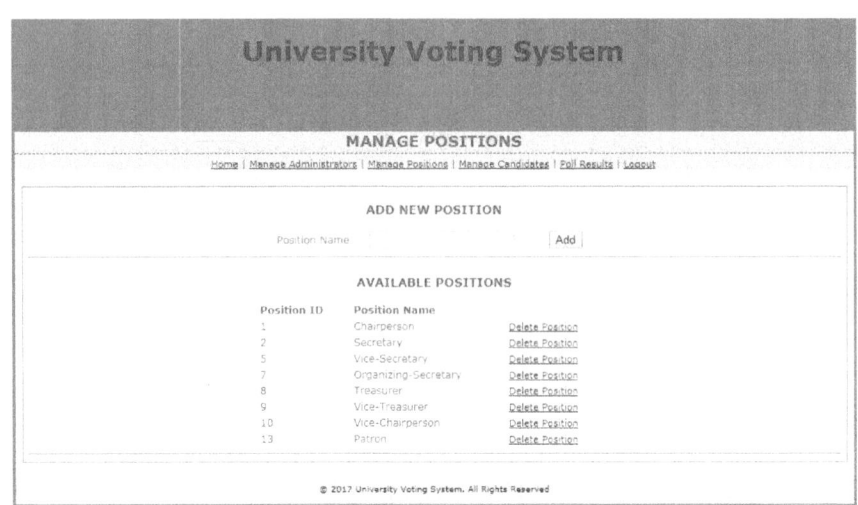

Figure 22. Manage Positions Page

4.3.6 Manage Candidates Page

This page enables the admin to add or remove the candidates that are contesting in the election.

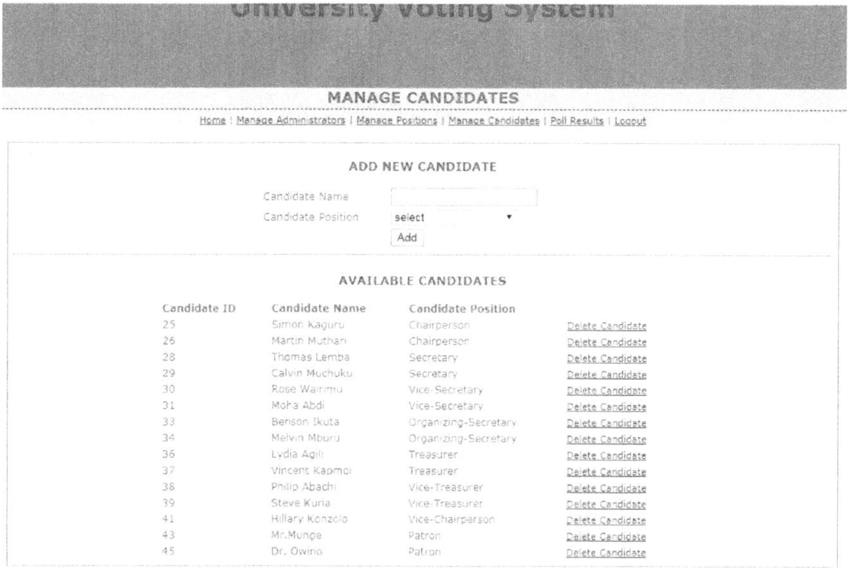

Figure 23. Manage Candidates Page

4.3.7 Manage Administrators Page

The admin is able to add more administrators into the UVS system in this page.

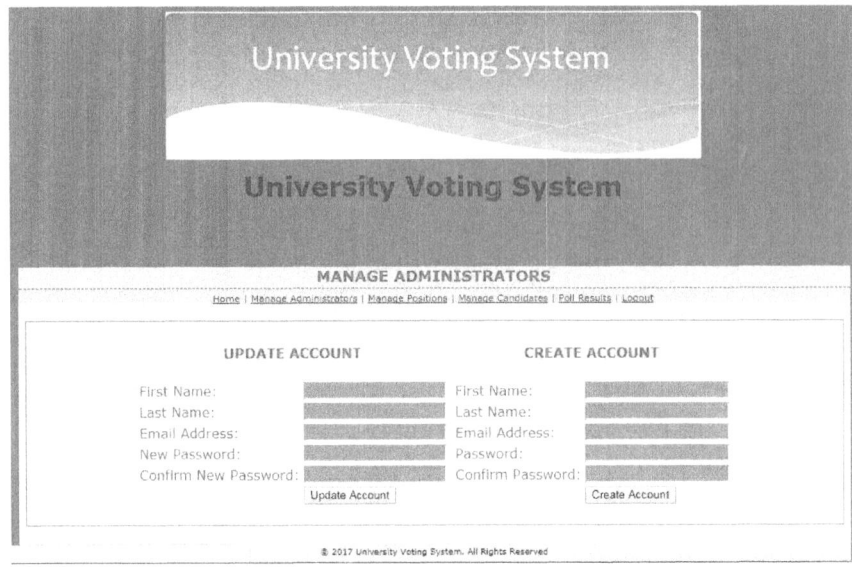

Figure 24. Manage Administrators Page

4.3.8 View Results Page

This page enables the admin to view the results of all the elections by selecting each and every position to view which candidate won the position.

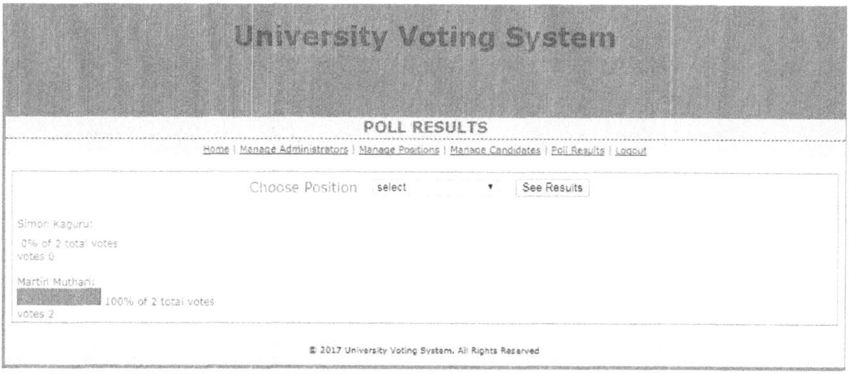

Figure 25. View Results Page

4.4 Results

For results gathering purposes, the developer created a user and an admin account to demonstrate how the UVS displays the outputs in order to decide which candidate wins the election. The accounts that were created had the following details:-

Admin

Email – admin@example.com

Password – admin

User

Email – user@example.com

Password – user

4.4.1 Voting Process

Once a user/student creates an account successfully in the UVS, he/she is then allowed to login.

Once logged in, the user should click the "current polls" panel in order to view the current

contesting candidates and then cast his/her vote on the same page.. For testing purposes, we

choose the candidates contesting on the Chairperson's seat.

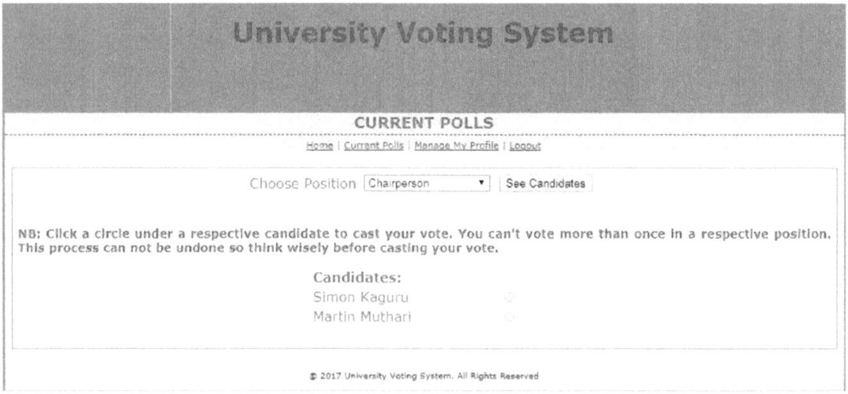

Figure 26. Voting Process

The candidates available were only two so the user in this case chooses "Simon Kaguru". Once

the vote is cast, the action cannot be re-done or re-edited.

4.4.2 Vote Tallying

Vote tallying is done by the administrator. The admin logs in the system with the details above and navigates to the "Poll Results" page. The admin chooses which position he/she would like to know the results of. In this case, the developer chooses the "Chairperson".

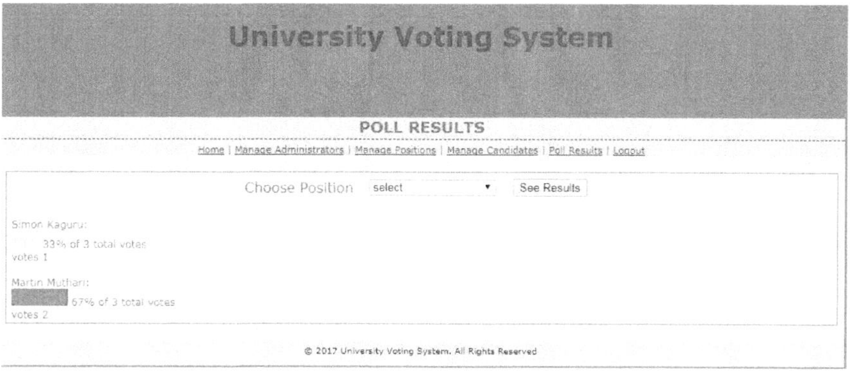

Figure 27. Vote Tallying

The admin can now be able to view the total votes cast and he/she cannot be able to change the data on the poll results.

CHAPTER FIVE

CONCLUSION, RECOMMENDATIONS AND FUTURE WORK

5.1 Conclusion

In this people, we have illustrated and identified the need to have an electronic voting system that systematically enables a student of a particular university to cast his/her vote through internet without going to voting booth and additionally registering himself/herself for voting in advance. As discussed, the UVS will be able to bridge the gap where students usually line up to vote for their preferred candidates in university elections by enabling them to vote online. The organizers of the election too will not have to tally the results manually as the UVS has the capability of tallying the results electronically and the organizers of the election will only access the UVS in order to view which candidate won the election.

The using of online voting has the capability to reduce or remove unwanted human errors. In addition to its reliability, online voting can handle multiple modalities, and provide better scalability for large elections in universities and also local elections. This will ensure that students in universities are provided with an electioneering process where they can elect their union leaders in a democratic manner. The system presented in this project paper offers a solution to many problems such as voter bribery, ballot stuffing, voter fraud and rigging which are prevalent in democratic process which utilize paper-based voting.

The results gathered by this paper illustrate that the UVS can be utilized effectively in providing a solution for learning institutions in the country. The human resource that is injected in conducting the elections will be reduced. The verification of the election can easily be conducted if a candidate is not satisfied but errors in the voting process are not likely to occur due to the security features provided by the UVS.

Although the system was developed with no significant emergence of errors, the developer faced some challenges in the development of the registration form that enables users to be registered in the UVS. The developer was not able to provide an external file containing the admission numbers of students which the system is supposed to counter-check with when registering new students/users. This challenge occurred because the UVS was locally hosted on a computer rather than when development of a web-based system is hosted online This challenge though a bit significant could not affect the voting process as per the regulations set that only students are able to cast their votes once the system is online.

Web-based portals or systems provide a great opportunity to institutions and entities which aspire to promote free and fair elections. The internet offers a wide range of technologies discussed on this paper and others that are not that be utilized in developing a web-based or a standalone system of voting that can be used in universities or even can be extended to national politics level by countries in the developing world with some modification.

5.2 Recommendations and Future Work

The objectives of this project was to review the existing/current system of voting in universities in Kenya and to also provide a solution that can enhance and promote fairness in elections that are held in universities rather than continue using the existing system which is regularly marred with irregularities in the voting process. This study therefore adopts the decision that learning institutions in Kenya and beyond should ensure that they install the UVS in their schools in order to enhance credibility of the elections. The project illustrates that the UVS can be used by any university which wishes to adopt an electronic means of voting. The UVS therefore can be used in each union body elections that are held in universities to avert any contention and manipulation results through acts such as voter bribery, voter fraud and ballot staffing.

The practicable future scope of the project includes the improvement in the security level of the system. This will ensure that errors that are likely to occur especially during the verification of voters are futile. Also, due to the adoption of smart phones especially by university students, a mobile application version of the UVS can be developed on the main operating systems i.e. Android and iOS as mobile apps tend to respond faster that web application as most data on mobile applications is stored locally on the mobile devices whereas web applications store their data on web servers. For this reason, data retrieval happens much faster on mobile applications than on web applications. Moreover, with the advancement in technologies, biometric measures such as face and finger print recognition algorithms could be applied to enhance security and improve credibility of online voting systems.

REFERENCES

Amirianzadeh M., Jaafari P., Ghourchian N. & Jowkar B. (2011). Role of Student Associations in Leadership Development of Engineering Students. Procedia - Social and Behavioral Sciences, 30, 382-385. http://dx.doi.org/10.1016/j.sbspro.2011.10.075.

Anand A. & Pallavi D. (2012). Analysis of an Electronic Voting System. International Journal of Modern Engineering Research, 2, 2631-2634.

Aziz, A. (2011). Online Election System : A Proposed System for Pakistan (Dissertation). Retrieved from http://urn.kb.se/resolve?urn=urn:nbn:se:uu:diva-159176

Chaum, D. (2004). Secret-ballot receipts: True voter-verifiable elections. IEEE Security & Privacy Magazine, 2, 38-47.

Commission of University Education (2014) Retrieved from http://www.cue.or.ke/index.php/services/accreditation/status-of-universities

Constitution of Kenya (2010). National values and principles of governance. Article 10 of the Constitution of Kenya, Retrieved from http://www.kenyalaw.org/lex/actview.xql?actid=Const2010#KE/CON/Const2010/chap_2/sec_10

Emaase P.M. (2011). E-voting readiness in Kenya: A case study of Nairobi county. (Thesis). Retrieved from http://erepository.uonbi.ac.ke/handle/11295/20094

Kalaichelvi V., & Chandrasekaran M. (2012). Design and analysis of secured electronic voting protocol. Asian Journal of Information Technology, 11, 50-55. doi: 10.3923/ajit.2012.50.55

Kohno T., Stubblefield A., Ribin A., & Wallach D. (2004). Analysis of an electronic voting system. IEEE Computer Society, 2(5) 27-40. doi:10.1109/SECPRI.2004.1301313

Lakshmi R., Nivya M. & Selvanayaki K. (2015). Student online voting system: International Journal of Trend in Research and Development, 2 (5) ,438-440

Nzoka J. & Ananda F. (2015). University Elections Management Portal. Innovative Systems Design and Engineering, 6(3), 34-35.

http://www.iiste.org/Journals/index.php/ISDE/article/viewFile/20600/21022

Shamos M. (1993). Electronic Voting - Evaluating the Threat. School of Computer   Science Carnegie Mellon University, 4-5

http://euro.ecom.cmu.edu/people/faculty/mshamos/CFP93.htm

Shamos M. (2004). Paper v. Electronic voting records – An assessment. School of ComputerScience Carnegie Mellon University, 4-5

http://euro.ecom.cmu.edu/people/faculty/mshamos/paper.htm

Universities Act (2012). Retrieved from http://www.cue.or.ke/index.php/universities-act-2012

Zhang, J. (2010). Development of e-commerce web application using WAMP. (Doctoral dissertation, San Diego State University). Retrived from http://sdsu-dspace.calstate.edu/handle/10211.10/640

APPENDIX

Appendix 1. Budget
Table 7. Budget

No	Item	Ksh
1	Laptop PC (Asus X 453M, Intel Pentium, 4GB RAM, 500 GB HDD)	30,000
2	Documenting the Project Proposal and Project Paper (Printing)	1000
3	Stationery [Pens, pencils, rough draft notebooks]	500
4	Research costs i.e. both Internet Access and other reserved materials in libraries such as newspapers	1000
5	Computer storage devices such as Flash disk, 2GB and CD ROMs	500
	Total Estimated Cost	**33,000**